AF375488

To the One and the ones who
show me what love means
every day. Thank you.
I love you.
J.T.

In this picture book, I alternate
between lines inspired by
1 Corinthians 13 (no specific version)
and my own playful rhymes in an
attempt to bring St. Paul's beautiful
exposition on love to children of all
ages. I hope you and yours love it.

(Biblical lines in **all black text**.)

Love is…

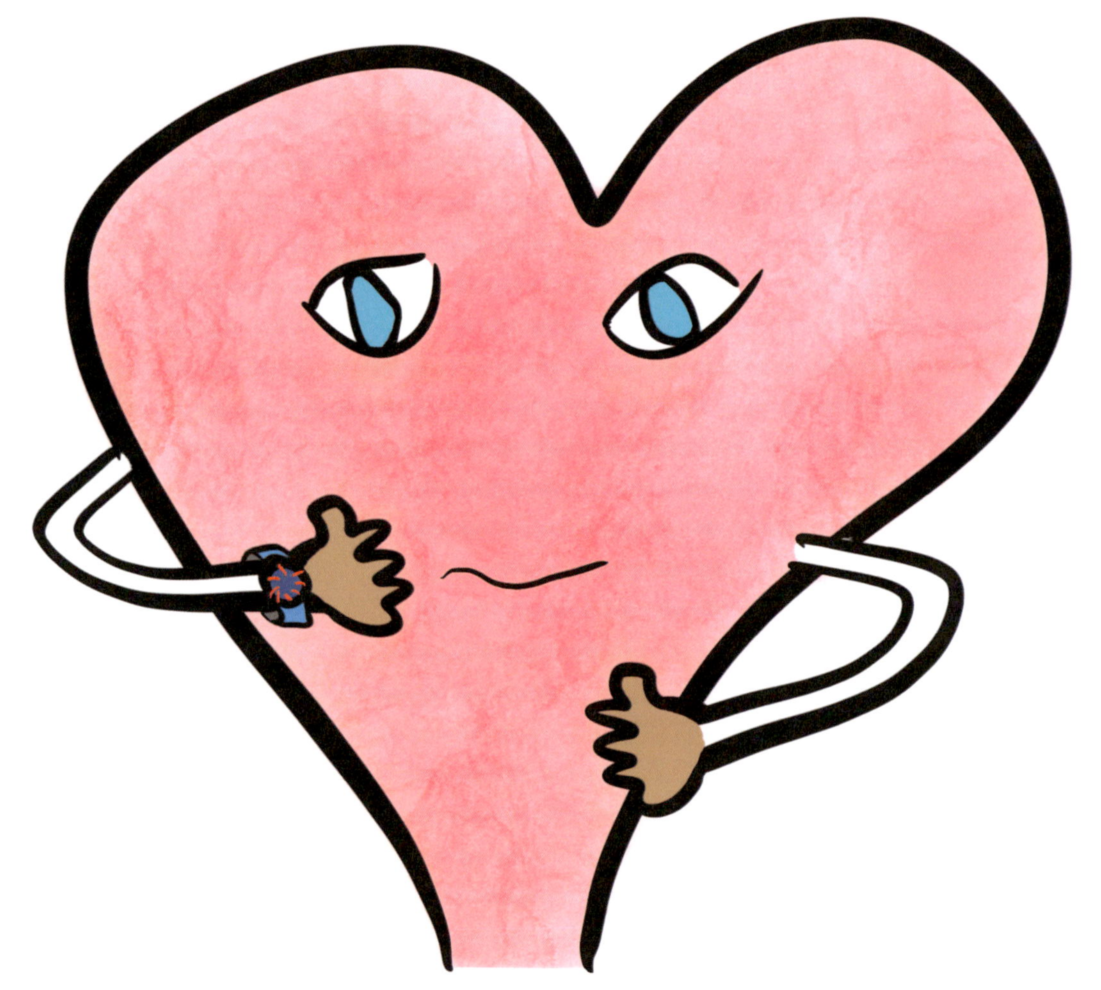

(Wait for it...)

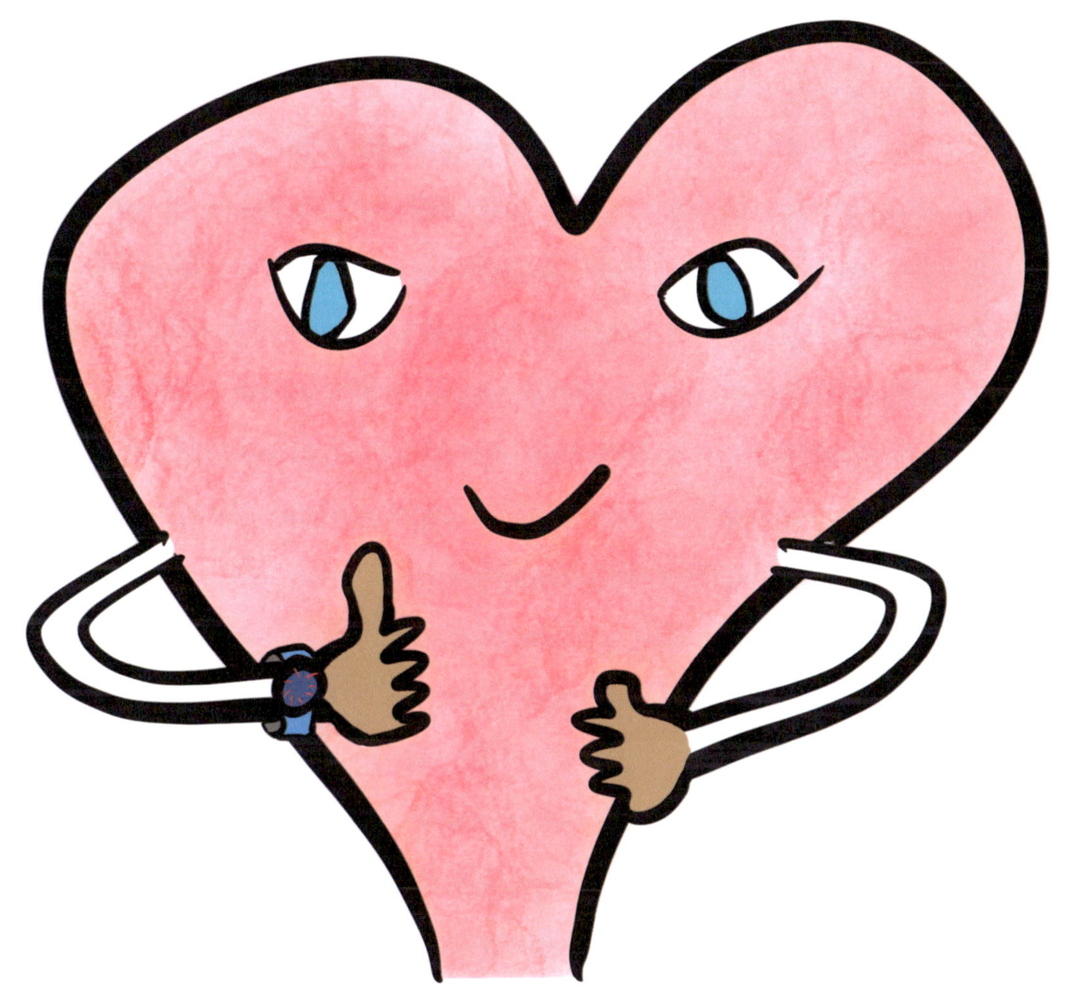

...patient!

Love is kind.

You might even say...

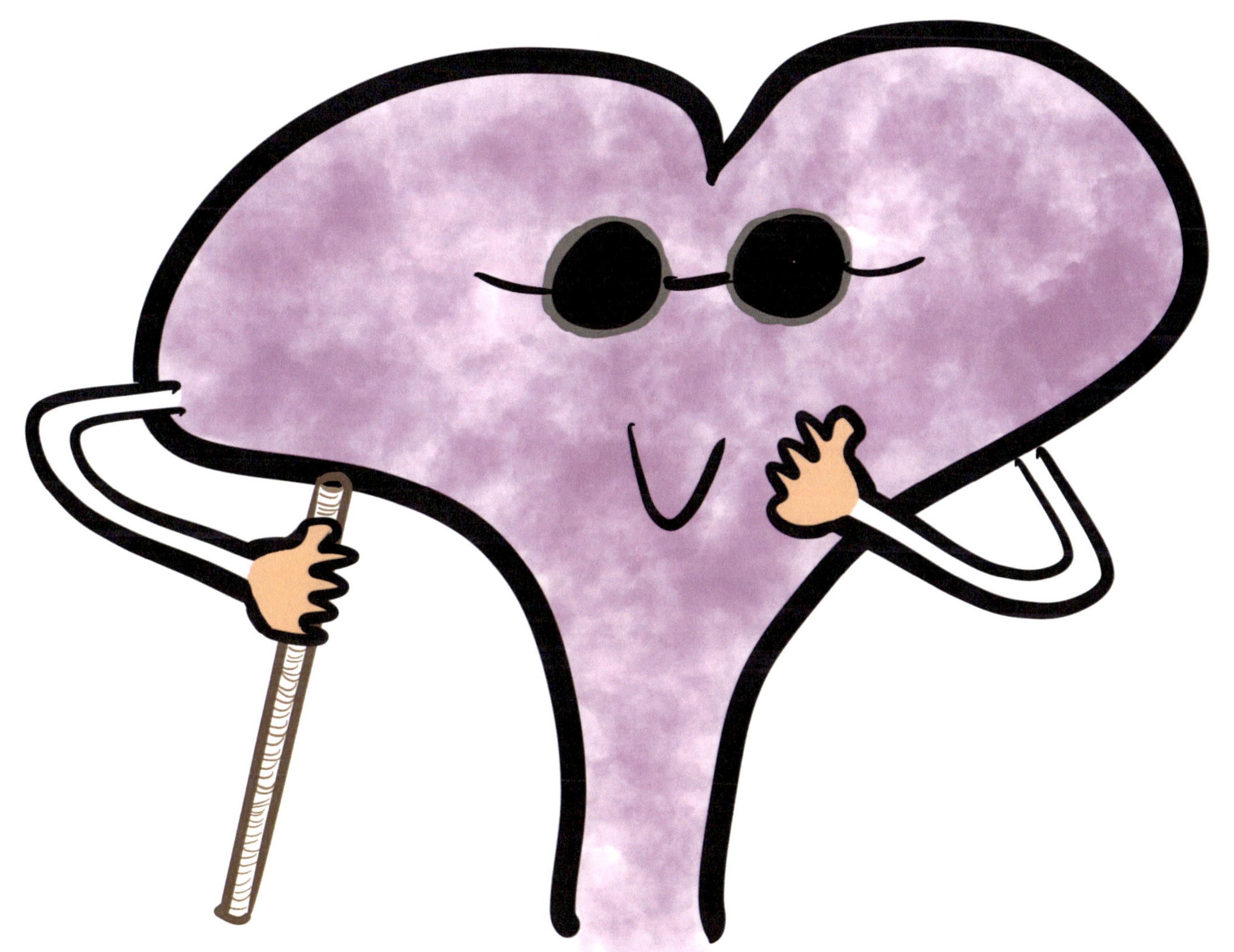

Love is blind.

Love never

envies.

Because *that's* how you make *enemies.*

It does not boast

even though it
cares the *most!*

It is not proud,

but it'll blush, if you
say it too loud.

It does not act rude,

or have a bad attitude!

It is not selfish,

and never acts

oafish.

Upsetting it is not easy…

since being mad
makes it *queasy*.

It does not dwell
on mistakes

no matter how many
redos it takes!

It doesn't delight in wrongdoing

nor does it talk while it's chewing!

It rejoices in the truth.

...I'll show you the proof!

It takes on *all* things

And will protect
you with a *sling*.

It trusts everyone...

...and everything
under the sun.

It always has high hopes,

no matter how many
times it's heard "nope."

It perseveres through everything

even a messy
ball of string!

Love **<u>never</u>** fails

It always **always** **always** prevails.

Without love...

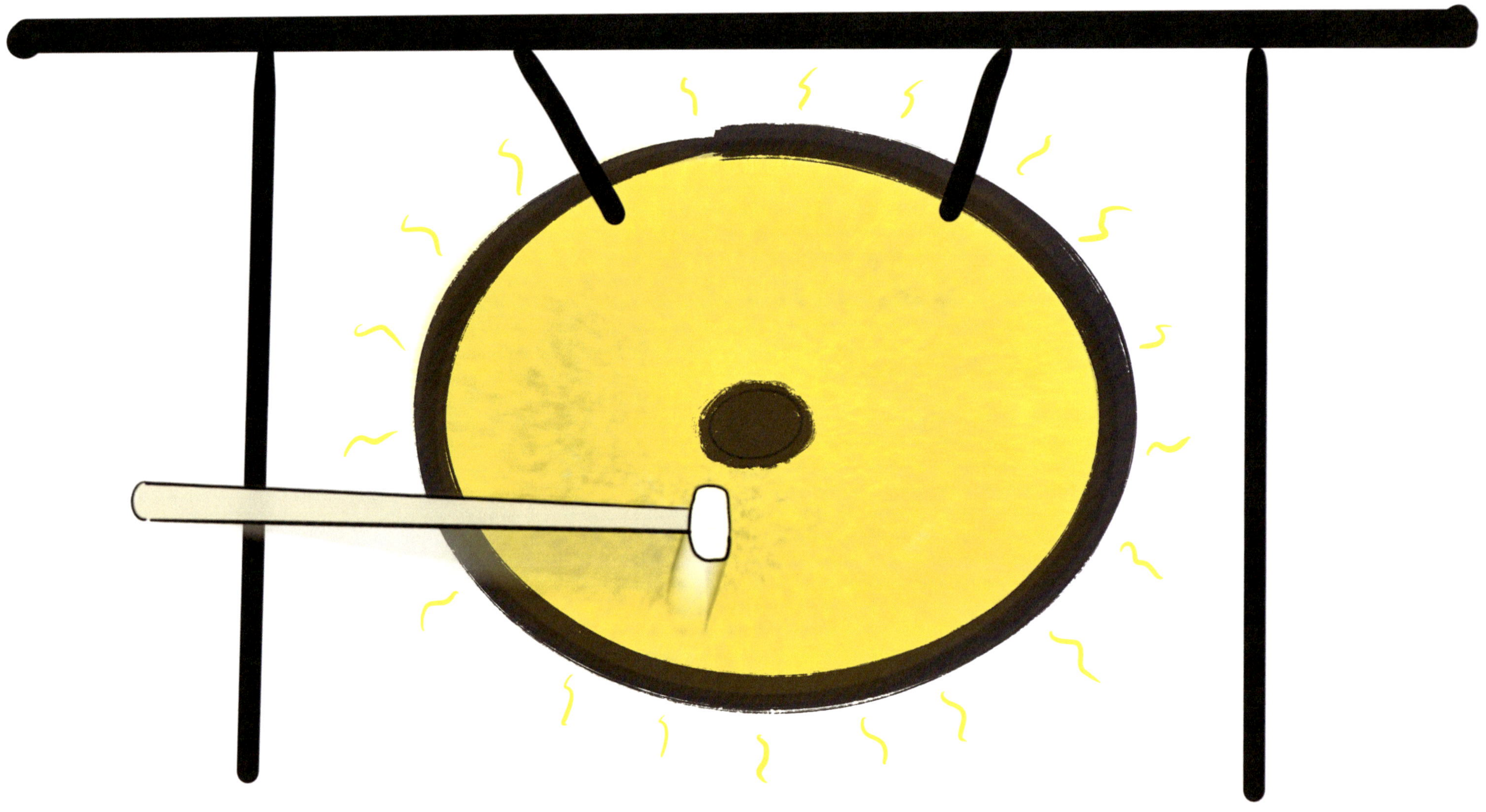
I am just a noisy gong!

Without love…

I am

nothing.

So, whatever you do,
love.

The end.

About the Author

Joe Tadros loves to see children smile, laugh, and learn. He created the **EZ-PZ Reading Book Series**™ to help children, including his own, learn to read their first words. He lives with his wife and 3 children in Southern California and attends St. Paul American Coptic Orthodox Church in Irvine.

Check out the
EZ-PZ Reading Book Series™